The Lady and
the Poet

The Lady and
the Poet

Michael Campbell

iUniverse, Inc.
New York Lincoln Shanghai

The Lady and the Poet

iUniverse books may be ordered through booksellers or by contacting:

iUniverse
2021 Pine Lake Road, Suite 100
Lincoln, NE 68512
www.iuniverse.com
1-800-Authors (1-800-288-4677)

ISBN-13: 978-0-595-40641-8 (pbk)
ISBN-13: 978-0-595-67822-8 (cloth)
ISBN-13: 978-0-595-85006-8 (ebk)
ISBN-10: 0-595-40641-6 (pbk)
ISBN-10: 0-595-67822-X (cloth)
ISBN-10: 0-595-85006-5 (ebk)

Printed in the United States of America

Contents

Introduction

When in search of the truth, we must examine the lies and fallacies of our every decision: *The Lady and the Poet* is a lyrical journey of love and life. It is my life's journey intertwined in a belief that the truth of happiness lies within the fears and joys of our denials. Although the readers may question my analogy and my description of love with these poems, no doubt they will find themselves entranced in the richness of these emotional stories. Whether these poems are actual accounts and events in my life or just fantasies and dreams, the reader is encouraged to find their own truth within the emotions they produce.

In recent years, I have traveled to several South American countries mainly for job assignments; however, these trips soon became my inspiration to write this book. In an environment where I am unable to communicate because of language barriers, I rely on my basic emotions. A smile, hand signals, and my many facial expressions say more than spoken words could ever say. Within the peaceful silence without words, I am not distracted by the faulty auditory signals of honesty.

A universal love is deeply embedded in the bonds of the commonalties of loving, friendships, and a self-defined happiness that everyone seeks in their life. This book offers readers the chance to reflect on events of their lives that can't be rewritten but can be resolved by the acceptance that life promises only experiences. It is our daily decisions that define the degree of happiness within our lives.

A percentage of the proceeds from this book are to be donated to the Sodavia Enterprise, LLC at www.sodavia.com to help fund a community support program in Ecuador. The program focuses on providing support services to indigenous communities in Ecuador. My affiliation with this program began with a visit to Ecuador in 2006. Within the next few months, I will relocate to Quito, Ecuador, to start a local volunteer community support division. Thank you for your support, and please visit the Web site for additional information about Sodavia Enterprise.

The Lady and the Poet

Woman, is the comfort of your heart within your sheets?
Has love become the night, and lust her stars?
And I, who have burned among your feats,
Must fall to dreams begrimed and spoiled.
You lie within the shadow of the foolish and young
To drink their words of pleasure, to believe, to want.
It's just a rude awakening; tomorrow it's alone
When pain becomes the love for the tears and the warmth.

And the poet sings, and the lady dances,
Lady apprentice, lady mannequin.
And the lady dreams and the poet recants.
Lady love, lady easy to commend,
It's a love for a lie, a game for the sport,
The lady and the poet.

Woman, once you stopped to drink, to talk with the poet,
To write in song the words of the love you sought to free.
Beyond the tide the sun shone, smiles brought you ashore.
The poet no longer wrote the rhyme, your gain became his weep,
And still the old are the wise, the young the fools to be,
To warm their lies in covered sheets, to hope this is the last,
To find that once again you burn within their heat.
The wise are eyes that see the question that's never asked.

And the poet sings and the lady dances.
Lady apprentice, lady mannequin.
And the lady dreams and the poet recants.
Lady love, lady easy to commend,
It's a love for a lie, a game for the sport,
The lady and the poet.

In the Arms of Peace

There are people everywhere living on the street.
We must find them shelter, their hunger we must feed.
We should take a little time from our busy day
To show them some love instead of turning them away.
I'm talking to the leaders of every nation.
Stop the oppression.
The world is in need of peace.

In the arms of peace, we'll see a world of unity.
There is so much harmony in the arms of peace.
Come on, let's talk, let's talk when we disagree.
You know we could be in the arms of peace.

There are children crying but we do not see their tears.
We fight each day for freedom and we still live life in fear.
What the world is in need of is for love to find a way
To change the hearts of people whose minds are filled with hate.
I'm talking to the people of every nation.
Stop the aggression.
The world is in need of peace.

Stop the wars; love your mother.
Stop the hate; love your father.
Stop the envy; love your sister.
Stop the fear; love your brother.
Stop the lies; love your neighbor,
Stop the crimes; love your nation.
Stop the destruction; love the world
Of young minds.

In the arms of peace, we'll see a world of unity.
There is so much harmony in the arms of peace.
Come on, let's talk when we disagree.
You know we could be in the arms of peace.

Stop the Wind

Blowing through my life these changes,
What a sacrifice you're claiming.

The sun will never rise again;
The night will keep me twisted till Amen
With words that cut so deep.
Who has the heart to watch me bleed?
But you can't take a chance;
You don't want to love;
You don't want to lead me on.

But, love I can hear
All the tears
Falling deep inside my heart.
Yes, I can hear
But I'd rather trust in faith,
And I'd rather believe
The truth is shown to those who seek.

And I can't stop the wind
Blowing changes through my life.
No, I can't stop the wind.
We must make the sacrifice.
For I can't stop the wind.
There'll never be a wrong that's right,
And I can't stop the wind.

Who's Heaven bound?
Sinners know where they are headed,
But what's in between?
How can it be
That the fruit became the master of the tree?

I'm trying to understand,
But I'm slipping every day
Into a gray
Shadow falling like the calm before the storm.

And I can't stop the wind
Blowing changes through my life.
No, I can't stop the wind.
We must make the sacrifice,
For I can't stop the wind.
There'll never be a wrong that's right
And I can't stop the wind.

I can't stop the wind;
I can't stop my heart;
I can't stop the love.
I can't stop the dark
From falling down on sleepless nights.
I can't stop the wrong that seems so right.
I can't stop the need;
I can't stop the fight.
I can stop the wind that blows my life.
I can't stop the want; I can't stop the fire;
I can't stop my faith in this warm desire.
I can't stop the love I feel for you.

The LAMP: Love and Affection Are My Only Perfection

Girl, I want to steal you
So that I can feel you
In the LAMP, the LAMP,
The magic LAMP.

You say there's no magic when I'm close to you,
No wonderful feelings that say love is true.
I say you're wrong; it was love from the start.
But how can I show you
While he's in your heart?

Girl, I want to steal you
So that I can feel you
In the LAMP, the LAMP,
The magic LAMP.

In the LAMP there's magic
That makes love appear.
It knows what your wish is
That I can fulfill.
Will you rub it for chance
Or just for romance?
Come and feel the magic
One rub can begin.

Girl, I want to steal you
So that I can feel you
In the LAMP, the LAMP.
The magic LAMP.

Rub it, rub it, rub it all down,
Love it, love it, rub it around.
Rub it, rub it, rub it all down,
Love it, love it, rub it around.

Girl, I want to steal you
So that I can feel you
In the LAMP, the LAMP,
The magic LAMP.

The LAMP is a room,
And the room's in my heart.
Love is a fire that rubbing will start.

One day I'm going to find a love that's free.
One day I'm going to find a love for me:
Somebody who'll give me lots of love,
Somebody who'll want my tender love,
Somebody who'll treat me oh, so fine,
Somebody who'll stay on my mind,
Somebody you'll want to be you,
That does the things you want to do.

Girl, I want to steal you
So that I can feel you
In the LAMP, the LAMP,
The magic LAMP.

I'll Still Be Your Fool

Outside this morning it's starting to rain.
You're packing your suitcase and I'm feeling the pain.
Is it that old friend you've known all your life?
The one that you ran to when things weren't right?
The radio plays while you're getting dressed;
All those love songs I now must forget.
Deep in the night where the dark meets the sky,
Shadows will come to me, whispering Why?

Don't say you love me with tears in my eyes.
Don't whisper you're sorry when you say good-bye,
'Cause I know it's over, yes, I know we're through,
But, Baby, I'll still be your fool.

Outside my door with the rain on your face,
You're hesitating; I'm hoping you'll stay.
You know he's waiting, and I know you'll go;
I only hope that you'll hold me once more.
No words are spoken, not even a try,
But you feel the hurt, see the pain in my eyes.
I wish I were dreaming and would wake up to find
That you're still beside me and love's still alive.

Kiss me a moment, then walk away.
Don't give me a second to beg you to stay.
'Cause I know your heart, and it's being untrue,
But, Baby, I'll still be your fool.

After your promises and after your lie
Have left you lonely and you realize
That love is forever, but never with you,
Maybe then I'll still be your fool.

Beauty Queens

Lady in the mirror, locked within your dreams,
Alice has lost her way from a beauty to a beast.
Too many nights have fallen, and they're bound to fall again.
So she takes away her loving and makes you wait in vain.

All of the young girls come to take a ride,
For beauty queens, through the looking glass,
To where Alice now resided.

Sing a song of a land where Alice once belonged.
Follow me to a fantasy; I'll make you queen for a day.
When years have grayed the yellow stone,
Someone else will take your place.

Alice's things get clearer when you shed away your dreams.
Skipping stones on a glossy lake don't make the wrinkles that you see.
It is lost for all time as a queen in Neverland.
Now you're chasing rainbows which will never end.

All of the young girls come to take a ride,
For beauty queens, through the looking glass,
To where Alice once resided.

Sing a song of a land where Alice once belonged.
Follow me to a fantasy; I'll make you queen for a day.
When years have grayed the yellow stone,
Someone else will take your place.

25th Street

Save me, oh, save me, I'm all out of dreams,
Walking through Heaven's zone on 25th Street.
Cars are the fashion parading under neon lights;
Faces through tinted glass tell their stories of life.
You stare, you frown and swear, and I smile back at you.
Billions of stars will fall before the night is through.

South of Main and Hollywood is 25th Street.
Liquid gold in glasses is always in our reach;
You can soar for days and days because the magic is good.
Feel the fire in our veins, we're the joke of the neighborhood.

I search to find a place to bury my head
Deep within my thoughts on the night edge.
Lovers sending messages through crystal eyes,
Passing the sights unknown we want to ask.
Give me another shot of that whiskey, man,
Fill up my dreamer's glass with my only friend.

South of Main and Hollywood is 25th Street.
Liquid gold in glasses is always in our reach.
You can soar for days because the magic is good.
Feel the fire in our veins; we're the joke of the neighborhood.

Daddy's Girl

Let's hear a cheer for the old family! Daddy must be
Proud of this girl now, proud that she's free
From a world of sin where colors blend.
Now that you're back, girl, back in his world,
Do you feel love was all a mistake?
Has he made you feel ashamed and disgraced?

What does it mean to be Daddy's girl?
Daddy gave up on you.
He didn't care, and he wasn't there.

Daddy's little girl is back at home;
There is no reason to carry on.
When you woke this morning,
Was there love in his eyes?
Was it all for you or just for his pride?
Daddy wants a world painted lily white;
Staying with the family sure feels right.
Daddy's little girl is back at home;
There is no reason to carry on this love.

There's only black, girl, and there's only white,
All through our lives.
The colors seemed bright when we were kids,
Free from the hatred of colors of skin.
Daddies should be more like us, sharing in love.
Maybe there'll be no suffering pain for
Those that are born to be shamed.
What does it mean to be Daddy's girl?

He gave up on you.
He didn't care, and he wasn't there.

Daddy's little girl is back at home;
There is no reason to carry on.
When you woke this morning, was there love in his eyes?
Was it all for you or just for his pride?
Daddy wants a world painted lily white.
Staying with the family sure feels right.
Daddy's little girl is back at home;
There is no reason to carry on this love.

Mamma Has Gone Away

When I was a little baby,
My Mamma rocked me in the cradle.
I remember crying in the night,
Her arms around me, holding so tight.
Mamma said, "Don't let life drive you crazy.
Believe in love, one day it will save you."

Years passed on, and Mamma passed on too.
I met a girl and carried her to wedding bells.
I tried to find the girl she'd love to meet.
Three years later I was back out on the street.
Mamma said, "A fool's lies will never die.
Trust in fate and always walk on Heaven's side."

I'm afraid to look out my window;
I'm afraid to walk down the street.
Mamma, tell me a story once more.
I'm afraid to go to sleep;
Mamma has gone away.

Now that I'm a man I can understand.
The roads of life can lead to nowhere land,
Where love is cold and heartbreaks are plenty,
I searched for dreams, to find there weren't any.
Mamma said, "There'll be a place in life
Where, my son, you've got to hold on tight."

In this life, we need a lasting courage
A kind of faith to believe it is all with it.
I tried to find the things I was taught as a child.
I knelt; I prayed and asked for my Mamma's smile.

Mamma said, "If the world is on your shoulder,
You'll find the strength to carry it as you grow older."

I'm afraid to look out my window;
I'm afraid to walk down the street.
Mamma, tell me a story once more.
I'm afraid to go to sleep;
Mamma has gone away.

Return to You in Graphics

Don't turn the lights out, it's still early;
There's still time to talk things out.
Blossom to me once more, my lady.
Night flowers are meant to sprout.
Don't take Heaven if you're leaving;
Hey, angel, solo it alone.
I'll meet you each night in stardom
Until you fall once more in my arms.

I return to you in graphics.
Misty water colors us there,
Framed in rims of our memories.
Seen through these eyes of glass,
The dust of heartache covers
The most wonderful love I had.

Don't turn lights on, no, lady;
I'm still lying in paradise.
Must the world come knocking so early
To steal my tomorrows from life?
Slicing through my dreams to peel me;
To reveal the love I've lost.
All that's left are heartaches in graphics,
Keeping dust off my walls.

I return to you in graphics.
Misty water colors us there,
Framed in rims of our memories.
Seen through these eyes of glass,

The dust of heartache covers
The most wonderful love I had.

I Just Can't Call It Love

Color me truthful. This is straight from my heart:
There's a feeling for all life's rewards.
Mine is from moments stolen from you.
Yours is to this love, to name just a few.

Shower you thankful. You're the fruit of the vine.
Our lives by their moments and memories design.
Time has no shadow and therefore no past
For rebuilding all of our hearts made of glass.

I just can't call it love,
Still I want to fall,
Into these dreams of us
Into the beauty of it all.

Label me guilty for feelings inside,
For dreams that are born when I look in your eyes.
Life keeps revolving, but I will review
The dreams that I've stolen, my heart's rendezvous.

I just can't call it love,
Still I want to fall,
Into these dreams of us
Into the beauty of it all.

This Is Your Song

Hey, Baby, I'm trying to make my stages;
Put my name up in lights.
You say I write you these silly love songs,
But one day, Baby, they'll mean a lot.
Maybe you think someday your lies will die,
But lies don't die, they just kick and scratch.
When you tell your friends that it's over,
Tell them you lost your lucky four-leaf clover.

Shine the bright lights on me.
Hear them calling my name.
Hey, Baby, this is your song;
See my glamour and fame.
For the fool on the street,
Hey, Baby, do you like your song?

Hey, Baby, we had to part as strangers,
Because there was no love in that icy smile.
When I made my debut on your stage,
You gave up on love and laughed a mile.
I'll play the world all your love songs,
To relate to these smiles and this pain.
Will you come back knocking at my heart, Baby,
Still playing that "I still love you" game?

Chauffeured cars, limousines,
Hollywood treats me fine.
Yeah, Baby, singing your song,
I cover *Stars* magazine.

Superstar feeling fine,
Sweet lady, just singing your song.

Pleasure Bones

Oh no. Don't start acting so grand.
You've played your part in some one-night stands.
Your eyes have been watching my sexy style;
The way I move really drives you wild.
You scan me all over from my head to my toes;
Your wishful thinking got you hotter than coal.
Desires burning, and I'm willing to bet
Tonight what you see is what you will get.

Come ride the night, I want to take you home;
I want to give you some of these pleasure bones.
There's a reaction that you've never known:
The satisfaction of my pleasure bones.
While love is burning, let your spirit run free.
I want to step into your fantasies.

Come on, Baby, don't put the night on the line.
You got to tell me if it's your place or mine.
I'm schooled in loving from A to Z,
There's nothing shy about me filling my needs.
I'm on the hunt, I'm going to take someone home.
Here's your chance to get these pleasure bones.
Rumor has it that life isn't fair,
But those are the breaks if you stay in that chair.

Come ride the night, I want to take you home;
I want to give you some of these pleasure bones.
There's a reaction that you've never known:
The satisfaction of my pleasure bones.

While love is burning, let your spirit run free.
I want to step into your fantasies.

Oh, Georgia

Where do we stand, Oh, Georgia?
Are we about to part?
I don't know, Baby, just what went wrong.
You can't tell me that your love for me is gone.

Like the sudden chills when fear is in the air,
My heart stood still when you told me how you felt.
I was thinking maybe of sharing a life,
In which you love me and you are my wife.

Please, please, Baby, throw me a line.
I'm sinking, Baby, for the very last time.
I'm going under in this sea of love;
The winds of pain have swept me overboard.
Oh, Georgia, is it a crime,
To hurt this loving heart of mine?
What happened to you, me, and us?
A promise to love and our vows trust.

Let the chips fall, oh, Georgia.
Another hand of bad cards
In the game of love we all will lose,
I had everything betting on you.
Now love seems like a whisper in the wind,
A memory constantly repeated by friends.
Deep inside me I know your love lives on.
I can't hold on knowing all hope is gone.

Please, please, Baby, throw me a line.
I'm sinking, Baby, for the very last time.
I'm going under in this sea of love;
The winds of pain have swept me overboard.

Oh, Georgia, is it a crime,
To hurt this loving heart of mine?
What happened to you, me, and us?
A promise to love and our vows trust.

Terri

I received your invitation, Terri,
To your wedding with a note I sadly read.
I thought time would never change you, Terri.
I thought love was always there for me.
Did he say he loved you more, Terri?
Did he promise he'll never go?
Was it that you got lonely, Terri,
And stepped in from the cold?

Terri, she's changing, she's being so new,
Turning to love from her solitude.
Choosing a man that she says she loves,
Trying to forget the way we once loved.

But does she really know?
Will she ever know
That I still love her so?

I remember the nights in Las Vegas.
I can still see your face at the table,
Running games of chance for the people.
My heart was cold and broken into pieces.
Then you came with angel eyes aglow,
Took my hand, and said you'd never let go.
You kissed my lips and wiped away my tears;
You broke the chains and freed my heart of fears.

Terri, she's changing, she's being so new,
Turning to love from her solitude,
Choosing a man that she says she loves,
Trying to forget the way we once loved.

But does she really know?
Will she ever know
That I still love her so?

A toast to you, Mrs. Terri Mason.
Congratulations on your recent marriage.
My gift to you with love, peace, and warmth
Is these dreams of old in a broken-hearted song.
Here's to you, the words and the melody,
A song of rhyme for the pain, then the miseries.
Your innocence was like children's playground joys,
But you traded love like they traded baseball cards.

Friends

I know that I have gotten myself
Hooked on love so many times.
I shared my life with so many strangers;
Too few have made me stay a while.
I built a world from pieces of a childhood
Without the love, without the care of sharing.
This doesn't mean I'm standing on the outside
Looking in, afraid of being friends, oh no.

I just want to hear that you will never go,
Because friends like us will never fade away.
If you're ever lonely, Baby, you just phone me;
Nights like that are why friends are made.
Yes, nights like this are why friends are made.

I'm going to go where the music takes me,
Going to sing till my songs desert me.
I've felt the rain falling like the tears of
The many hearts I broke along the way.
If I never say that this love is real,
It'll never have to end someday.
For you, my friend, this love is special,
Believe in me, have faith in what I'm saying, girl.

I just want to hear that you will never go,
Because friends like us will never fade away.
If you're ever lonely, Baby, you just phone me;
Nights like that are why friends are made.
Yes, nights like this are why friends are made.

In a Nuclear World

I don't want to be on the Earth when she rumbles,
When those bombs start falling, oh no.
I don't want to be on a hill in a chapel;
I don't want to be here at all.
I don't want to see the eyes of the disbelievers;
I don't want to see their tears at all.
I don't want to feel the pain of radiation,
Because, people, you know it burns.
I want to keep my days in the sunshine;
I want to keep my family sane.
All this talk you talk about fighting,
Come talk to me, don't you want to explain?

In a Nuclear World,
You've got the power in your hands.
What demands
Will make you push the button, make your stand,
To rain down radiation on the lands,
In a Nuclear World?

I don't want to be underground in a shelter,
When the hungry start crawling, oh no.
I don't want to be with those who take to killing
Just to feed their hungry mouths.
Their faces will show all the terror
When the blood runs cold in their veins.
Will you talk of peace through victories?
Destroying the lands, you seek to gain.
I want to keep my days in the sunshine;
I want to keep my family sane.

All this talk you talk about fighting,
Come talk to me, don't you want to explain?

In a Nuclear World,
You've got the power in your hands.
What demands
Will make you push the button, make your stand,
To rain down radiation on the lands,
In an Nuclear World?

Circles of Friends

Some people haven't felt a burning love that
Makes some return to knock on love's doors.
They're waiting, hoping that they will find
The answer we've found living inside
This circle of friends.

If there's a load you cannot bear,
Friends are always there.
Just reach out your hands.
You'll feel the strength of
Circles of friends.

Years can't erase what's captured in photographs.
With one look at them, feelings come rushing back.
Memories of special things are made in our hearts;
Make one today. Record all
In circles of friends.

If there's a load you cannot bear,
Friends are always there.
Just reach out your hands.
You'll feel the strength of
Circles of friends.

No island can endure the wind and the waves alone.
There are trees to calm the angry wind.
The rocks break the waves in the storms.
People, like islands, don't stand alone.
We need to live all lifelong
In circles of friends.

Remember, friends will cushion the fall.
They're always there when we call
On circles of friends.
Call, call, call on circles of friends.

Killing Those Feelings

It used to be we'd have a conversation;
We'd talk about our old friends and relations.
You tell me that things have changed.
Is this a point in the game?
Where you turn and I turn, and
We both just walk away.
Hell, I know things can't be
What they used to be, no, Baby.
I thought this friendship
Would last for eternity.
God bless that child of ours,
May she forever smile.
Could be that she is the only one to pay
For our killing those feelings of yesterday.

I can see that there'll come a day
When we'll stand face to face.
Embarrassed by the silence, we'll look away.
Although we'll try, there'll be no words to say,
When we're killing those feelings of yesterday.

I think you got yourself in a lonely situation.
What a sacrifice you make for a little appreciation.
Am I to read between the lines?
What is there for me to find?
A cross to bear for the pain out there
On a road, that led us from friends.
Is it love that makes you want
To do these things, oh, Baby?
You once saved me from the fire;
Will you let me cool your flames?

Besides, we've got to take the time
To explain to the little child
Of things to come now that we've gone
And paved the way
To killing those feelings of yesterday.

I can see that there'll come a day
When we'll stand face to face.
Embarrassed by the silence, we'll look away,
Although we'll try, there'll be no words to say,
When we're killing those feelings of yesterday.

Lovers to Friends

I just stopped to say hello.
You asked me not to go.
There's a silence darkness brings to life.
What are friends for if we can't sacrifice?
I gave my life, and I bled for you.
We talked, we laughed, we tried
To touch a world that's deep inside.
I knew the words came very hard,
I took the blows, I played my part,
I gave my life, and I bled for you.

Now I find that I cannot fade
The memories of the love we made.
Friends who said they cared,
Nights we sometimes shared,
Brought the pain of anticipating
The love that would keep me waiting
For the warmth you seldom gave.
It was dressed in love's masquerade.
I liked those nights that were aflame.
I liked the way you called my name
In the dark when you held me tight,
Our friendship was far from sight.

When I stumbled, I came tumbling in.
I fell into your life, I fell for a friend.
We took a chance, we went too far,
We chanced a kiss, a touch in the dark.
You threw the stone, and I took the bruise.
We stopped the world, we stopped the night,
We broke the vows of friends, it felt so right.

How are friends supposed to carry on when
Lovers fade away at dawn?
You threw the stone, and I took the bruise.

Now I can't fade away
From all the love we made,
Friends who said they cared,
Nights we sometimes shared,
Brought the pain of anticipating
The love that would keep me waiting,
The warmth you seldom gave.
It was dressed in love's masquerade.
I liked those nights that were aflame.
I liked the way you called my name
In the dark when you held me tight,
When friends were so far from sight.

Love, You and Me

I sat to unwind
All my feelings of today.
Sure the road has too many bridges;
Don't let heartbreak get in your way.
If the story must have an ending,
Write it well, and sign it with love.
If your question is What will our lives be?
My unspoken answer is love.

Baby, my heart's afire.
It's getting to me.
I walked into this dream
That is destined to be
Love, you and me.

Don't give in too easily
To those calls of yesterday.
Some will tell you love's a game, girl;
Don't examine the rules of play.
When you're tired, rest your head, love,
Over the rainbows where bluebirds fly.
Je t'aime, my lady. Somewhere I've read
It means I love you and that's no lie.

Baby, my heart's afire.
It's getting to me.
I walked into this dream
That is destined to be
Love, you and me.

Can You Share Your Pillow

There's a face in the mirror that I don't want to see.
It's been hanging around for days, refusing to let me sleep.
The silly life, the problems too rough to talk out,
So I call on you, my friend; I know you'll understand.

Can you share your pillow
With a broken heart?
Can you move real close now,
And take me in your arms?
Can you share your pillow
And meet me half the way
To a love that's living
Between the masquerades?

The world seems so much colder when love has left my life,
But here you always wait for me. One day I'll make it right.
You'll spend no more nights alone, waiting for me to show,
But tonight I need your arms. Come and hold me close.

Can you share your pillow
With a broken heart?
Can you move real close now,
And take me in your arms?
Can you share your pillow
And meet me half the way?
To a love that's living
Between the masquerades?

Feel the Music

Are you running in a circle?
Are you running out of dreams?
Do you find that life's a habit
Just a repeating movie theme?
Is the midnight like a stranger,
Giving you unfriendly vibes?
There's a message in my music
Asking you to come alive.

Can you hear my music playing
When the silence fills the air?
Do you reach for empty spaces
Just to realize no one's there?
Do the shadows dance in water
While reflecting life's abuse?
There's a freedom in my music
And my music is the truth.

Do your dreams come into vision
In the gleaming midnight lights?
Did the darkness tell you secrets
Until morning danced in sight?
Has Death brought you his angel
To sing at Dreamer's Prom?
If there's Heaven in my music,
Then Hell is in my song.

Romeo and Snow White

He felt the neon burning, felt it hot against his skin,
All the street songs kept on blowing through the bars of boozer gin.
The night she teased immensely to the angels on the block,
Walking in a crowd of beggars when the city doors unlock.

The night was so familiar, raining down with social class,
As all the painted ladies danced behind the picture glass.
There's a graveyard in the city where she's buried all her ghosts,
Where the stories on the gravestones have been read from coast to coast.

All the cars were kneeling to their glowing neon God,
Hanging on a cable shining brightly in the dark.
No one seems to notice Romeo and Snow White's hearts,
Sinking deep into desire in the night in Central Park.

Snow White had played a beauty, played it till the mirror cracked.
Seven men in seven stories was the cost to get it back.
Romeo in wisdom wrote the rhymes of washroom poets.
The words were never his but were of the life he wrote.

Snow White was so pretty in the moonlight golden glow,
When she fell into a story, when she fell for Romeo.
As the night became a tunnel and the darkness filled their eyes,
The sounds of wonder filled the air, and sounds of passersby.

The cars all kept on kneeling to their glowing neon God,
Hanging on a cable shining brightly in the dark.
No one seems to notice Romeo and Snow White's hearts,
Sinking deeper in desire, foraging through Central Park.

Romeo drank a grail of notions when he and Snow White met.
He bared a curse of memories of his sweet Juliet.

The night befell this lover's quest as chance did set the stage,
For Romeo to play and sing his story's serenade.

Some have died to feel the freedom, this freedom of the soul,
When Snow White drank the meaning of the stories that he told.
Hand and hand they seemed to touch the middle of the crest,
Where night and day can fall away and each is at his best.

Now the cars were stopping for their glowing neon God,
Swinging on a cable showing dimly in the dark.
Everyone is seeing Romeo and Snow White's hearts,
Burning brightly with desire, burning life in Central Park.

Easy Gamblers

Through the clouds of smokers' cigarettes,
The cards are drawn and we make our bets.
Easy gamblers, we are easy gamblers.

The drink on the table is my lady.
The stars on the jukebox play for free.
When the players raise, you've got to cover it,
Fold, or bluff, or see the leading bet.
Easy gamblers, we are easy gamblers.

Easy gamblers never fold.
They chase a lady queen as night grows old.
Easy gamblers, you're betting with spades.
Now the cards have fallen, pay the debts you've made
To the gamblers, winning easy gamblers.

Soon the tavern shows the signs of emptying.
The bartender brings us our final drinks.
The cards are old. Break out a brand new deck.
Play your every game with no regrets.
Easy gamblers, we are easy gamblers.

The innkeeper sweeps and locks the barroom,
As he sings a song you knew in school.
The cards will tell the story
Through the night of gambler's glory.
Easy gamblers, we are easy gamblers.

Through the night, you'll find the reason
To play cards in every season.
Easy gamblers, we are easy gamblers.

Easy gamblers never fold.
They chase a lady queen as night grows old.
Easy gamblers, you're betting with spades.
Now the cards have fallen, pay the debts you've made.
Easy gamblers, we are easy gamblers.

Mannequin Woman

Give me a line of communication.
We disagree so much; I wonder why.
You're so very high on consolation;
I take rejection as the need to try.
Our split decisions make the headlines.
My friends read the pain all over my face.
I'm locked in a feeling of doing my time
In a broken heart that's such a lonely place.

I won't be packing sorrow.
I won't be packing pain.
I won't be tracking memories
Through the regions of my brain.
Mannequin woman, no mannequin woman.

Here I am standing on a winding road.
I can't see ahead or what lies at the end.
Although I once saw the love, felt a belief within.
Today my heart is it filled with doubt
A hollow thought of what might have been
Those precious eyes show the beauty you bear.
They show the graves of many, so many who tried
To gain your love, but they were left in despair.
Your heart's too cold, and your words are all lies.

I won't be packing sorrow.
I won't be packing pain.
I won't be tracking memories
Through the regions of my brain.
Mannequin woman, no mannequin woman.

Cruise Master

Touch down, easy landing, refuel;
Thought love would cruise forever with you.
The world was just a stone at our feet.
The stone grew a love that forced down the machine.
Cruise master, cruise on.

On the ground you longed for that feeling of flight,
For the sound of the wind in the darkness of night.
You missed the wind, missed the sound of my wings
Standing on the strip looking for my machine.
Cruise master, cruise on.

Cruise master, autopilot,
Come on, pretty Baby, you can ride my jet.
My instruments are checked, I'm at my cruising speed,
My radar's on your loving, Baby, hot on your needs.
Cruise master, cruise on.

My compass says I'm headed down south;
A southern night for a star that burns out.
I'll fill up your space, I'll orbit your dreams
Through the sound of speed, and make love on my wings.
Cruise master, cruise on.

My sonar plays the sounds from the strip tonight;
My lady is back and wants to cruise on my flight.
She missed this super love, missed my super jet,
A love that's hypersonic they will never forget.
Cruise master, cruise on.

Cruise master, autopilot,
Come on, Pretty Baby, you can ride my jet.
My instruments are checked, I'm at my cruising speed,
My radar's on your loving, Baby, hot on your needs.
Cruise master, cruise on.

Rolling On

She was only seventeen but somehow she stole my heart.
In a bar, on a stool, she played alone on her guitar.
As she sang her sweet love songs, she looked at me and smiled.
Looking into her eyes I knew I'd be there for a while.

Her songs kept rolling on, just rolling on,
Rolling on away.
My heart kept rolling as she strummed,
Rolling as she played.

Her beauty touched my soul that first time she looked at me.
In her song she sang of love as I watched endlessly.
I had eight years on her, but she was still a lady.
In my mind, I dreamed of her love as her songs filled my ears.

Her songs kept rolling on, just rolling on,
Rolling on away.
My heart kept rolling as she strummed,
Rolling as she played.

In her charm was innocence, the bliss of the young.
Why was I forgetting the time, losing my heart in her songs?
I spent the night loving her, until the breaking dawn.
Years have passed and I still feel the magic in her songs.

My life keeps rolling on, just rolling on,
Rolling every day.
My heart keeps rolling on, feeling her charm,
Hearing the songs that she played.

Party Poops

When the lights go down
On this side of town,
You put on your dancing feet.
We settle back
And don't approve
Of your rhythm beat.
If the music sounds good,
Then knock on wood,
But we'd rather hear a different beat.

Because we're members of the party poops,
We don't wear dancing boots.
We're strictly nine to five.
"Have a cup of tea" is how we socialize.
We are the party poops,
Standing wall to wall.

You can stand us up,
And you can watch us fall.

You know we are plain;
We do not rock or sing.
We do not tap our feet.
We're always in by ten.
And then we're fast asleep.
You play your music loud,
For that cranked up crowd.
We wish they'd dance to a softer beat.

Because we are members of the party poops,
We don't wear dancing boots.
We're strictly nine to five.

Drinking tea is how we socialize.
We are the party poops,
Standing wall to wall.
You can stand us up,
And you can watch us fall.

Let Me Dream On

Unfolding, unwinding, I'm falling in dreams.
I'm fine when I find your beauties unseen,
When I chance to romance by candlelit eyes,
Heaven flows with feeling rejoicing inside.

A stolen kiss through a mist enchanted by love,
Casts this magic spell when you fell off wings from above.
No spoken words have I heard, yet I'm not alone.
My eyes are tight, don't wake the night, just let me dream on.

Fantasies are mysteries revolving the truth,
Arranging things, explaining dreams, when we introduce.
In darkness arms with twilight charms, we danced with the moon,
Broken play, by light of day, when sun starts to bloom.

Once again, I'm back with friends, sitting on a shelf,
Until I find a spot that's blind to dream in myself.
So stop the wind, hate a friend, let the world be reborn,
Make-believes and fantasies will let me dream on.

Oblivion

Sometimes I get lonely
For good-looking women
Just like you.
Oh, Baby, just like you.
My heart won't waste time.
I'll take the steps to make you mine.
Say you love me too.
Say your love is true.

I was standing underneath your window
With the roar of angry thunder.
Were you being true?
Who was pleasing you?
Sometimes it doesn't seem right.
When you lose a love, they steal her in the night,
And it's a hurting thing, when you have no dreams.

Don't blame the people, I say.
Life is a winding highway.
Caught on that byway,
Lost without love,
Hold onto your dreams, I say.
Help me through my troubled days.
I don't want my life to fade away
Into oblivion.

I have the sun on my shoulder
And a beard that's ten days old now.
When did you feel the chance
To still romance?
My jeans are somewhat dusty,

And my shoes are badly worn.
Would you want them too?
You don't play by rules.

I was standing underneath your window,
Feeling like an organ grinder.
When his monkey passed on,
He stopped playing his songs.
You know sometimes I feel abused,
Like I've been kicked by your shoes,
Born to lose, born in a noose.

But don't blame the people, I say.
Life is a winding highway.
Caught on that byway,
Lost without love,
Hold onto your dreams, I say.
Help me through my troubled days.
I don't want my life to fade away
Into oblivion.

Ophelia Love

She was a lady, fresh like the morning.
She was a lady, free as the wind.
I was a captain, a lonely captive;
She was a sailor on her voyage of love.
Together we made it, soft like the silence,
Through the eyes of sensuality.
All were my wishes, but she didn't notice.
Her thoughts were of him as she danced in my arms.

Ophelia, love,
Chained by your hopes and dreams.
Ophelia, love,
Awash in lies, you'll never come clean,
Ophelia, love.

Down from a distance, echoes kept calling,
For answers to questions too young to know.
When I felt the magic, I wanted to kiss her.
Her eyes told the story. Sometimes you lose.
Down around the border of love and loneliness,
She keeps a close account of her heartbreak in jest.
No one gets the autumn, the spring, or the summer.
All that's left is winter blowing coldly in her eyes.

Ophelia, love,
Chained by your hopes and dreams.
Ophelia, love,
Awash in lies, you'll never come clean,
Ophelia, love.

Reynolds Town

Some cold day they going to lay me down,
Nail up my coffin in Reynolds town.
I don't like trouble, so I walk away.
I don't like a hassle if my heart's to pay.

My baby gave me trouble. I caught her with that man,
And if love is for the killing, then a lover never hangs.
Now it's under cover when I'm on the street.
I don't want anyone catching hold of my ID.
Now every day takes me to a different place.
I'm tired of running, and it shows on my face.

I wish I were back in Reynolds town,
Shopping on the boulevard, cruising around.
A hundred times I've shut the old place down,
From west of Monticello to the north of Brown.
There weren't no hassles and their beds were warm.

Me and Billy Ray really had some fun,
And every day we could always be found
Living the good life down in Reynolds town.

These old bones ain't gonna rise one day.
I'm going to keep my trouble till my judgment day.
I'll ride every highway again and again.
Her rocky shoulders are my only friend.

My baby took a lover down in Reynolds town;
My heart was kind of troubled so I laid them down.
I watch for private eyes, bounty hunters, and thieves.
The FBI, the CIA, they all want me.

Now every day takes me to a different place.
I'm tired of running and it shows on my face.

I wish I were back in Reynolds town,
Shopping on the boulevard, cruising around.
A hundred times I've shut the old place down,
From west of Monticello to the north of Brown.
There weren't no hassles and their beds were warm.

Me and Billy Ray really had some fun.
And every day we could always be found
Living the good life down in Reynolds town.

You'll Need Me

There will be time enough tomorrow.
That's what they told us all our lives growing up.
Patience is a virtue that I don't care for,
If it means waiting for a change to come.
You've got to live for the moment and die for the chance.
Be brave when you're hurting, and maybe then
You'll need me.

I love the way you are, Baby.
Don't change a thing about you.
Baby, always stay around me,
Loving me all the way through my life.
You'll need me.

Now is the time; the place is tomorrow
For planting our dreams and watching them grow.
When you reach out for love, they'll put your heart in a harness.
They're going to try to tame you, stop the stallion from running.
You'll need someone, Baby, you'll need someone strong.
When you find you're hurting, when you find you're alone.
You'll need me.

I love the way you are, Baby.
Don't change a thing about you.
Baby, always stay around me,
Loving me all the way through my life.
You'll need me.

Standing in the Sun

The knowledge of Hell is in your eyes.
The power of war is at your side.
The freedom of life hastens you;
Let's zoom on a rocket to the moon.
Hang-ups are spreading, let's cover our souls.
We sacrifice our people for the power of gold.
Let's gravitate, while life accelerates.
Let's fly beyond the stars, to Mars.

Standing in the sun, I'm going to catch my shine.
I hope it purifies this world's dirty mind.
Standing in the sun, I'm going to be someone.
Won't you take my hand and sing my song?
Standing in the sun, naked as my birth,
Why can't we live together here on Mother Earth?

The mirror of time reflects its past;
The cycle of life moves way too fast.
Your reason for being puzzles you.
Let's all just meditate, let's escape.
The fires of Hell burn at Heaven's gate.
The showers of love can only conquer hate.
Scoop the ashes from the ground,
Turn to the wind, and blow, my friend.

Standing in the sun, going to catch my shine,
Hope it purifies this world's dirty mind.
Standing in the sun, going to be someone,
Won't you join my hand and sing my song?

Standing in the sun, naked as my birth,
Why can't we live together here on Mother Earth?

Like Misty Waters

Like misty water, my life is all clouds,
Roads that are closed, parks without crowds.
Faceless dreams through old broken glass,
Buried love awakened from a forgotten past.
Like misty water flowing through the wild,
Running deep in my mind so calm and so mild.
Someone stirred the bottom, clouding my view,
And it brought back these old memories of you.

Like misty water that has no place or destiny,
I've faltered, lost inside a lonely heartbeat.
I know that this moment will be short, it won't last,
When the misty water begins to flow past.
These loving thoughts of you and my misty eyes
Keep the misty water running deep inside.

Like misty water that's cool and wet,
The doors of winter and the autumn crest,
The eyes of Mars that spy a lover's quest,
These memories of you fill the emptiness.
Like misty water that's muddy and deep,
Like the morning dew and summer heat,
Eyes that are blind and hands that can't touch,
These dreams of old can bring back so much.

Like misty water that has no place or destiny,
I've faltered, lost inside a lonely heartbeat.
I know that this moment will be short, it won't last,
When the misty water begins to flow past.

These loving thoughts of you and my misty eyes
Keep the misty water running deep inside.

Our Home

Billions of dreams, ages of loves ago,
We played hide-and-seek in worn-out clothes,
On concrete parks, in empty cars,
Down by the neighborhood store.
Through books, we built our hopes and dreams
From the memories of our childhood scenes.
We set our goals and added "Mr." to our names.
We gave up our homes, the streets, and the gang.
We packed our bags with newly found hopes,
For respect and wealth we found in banker's notes.

Marble-laid skies through clouds
Of mystic graves.
We chance the fate of falling stars
For an honest day's wage.
Flowing crystal dreams can take us far,
Way beyond twilight's zone.
Still we find the best of who we are
On our return home.

We left behind the huge birch tree
Where children still carve their names.
The street lights replaced the oil lamp poles,
The landmark of the old gang.
For we are now shirt and tie, executive prone,
Appointed to this task for the trading of our homes.
So bring on the supermarkets, highways, and malls,
The small towns, cold beds, and rooms with bare walls.
Because our homes now lie where we can find
Tranquillity within a void aloft in our minds.

Marble laid skies through clouds
Of mystic graves.
We chance the fate of falling stars
For an honest day's wage.
Flowing crystal dreams can take us far,
Way beyond twilight's zone.
Still we find the best of who we are
On our return home.

Lonely City

Lonely city where a lover weeps,
Have you seen my baby?
With her smiling face,
She was such a lovely lady.
The ever-changing faces of love
Brought a new joy to her
And left me no room to compete.
Now in the darkness of the night,
I roam the streets.

Lonely hides the love
That I so rightfully earned,
Down in the dark black pits of night
Where the lights of love don't burn.
I hear the twelve-o'clock bells,
So I'll give it one more try.
I search one more bar,
One more hotel.

My love for her will not die.
It'll be forgotten like an old love song,
Forgotten, but never gone.
What will become of my broken heart
After my unsuccessful search?
Will I ever again know her
Sweet kisses, her words of love,
Or her warm tender touch?

Be a Friend Today

Attention, attention, we've searched the world over,
Looking for a love today.
We're voices of pleasure here to deliver
Love in a special way.
We're hoping you'll join us, stand up, applaud us,
And feel as we do in our hearts.
Shine on your children their love for tomorrow.
Teach them love is not so hard.

We all know a smiling face
Can make this world a better place.
We all know it's true that each of you
Can make a friend today.

Attention, attention, we're posting a notice
For you to come join our ranks.
We're soldiers of pleasure, here to convince you
That love is like cash in the bank.
Our music will move you, we're going to prove to you,
That we can shed their world of hate.
Hey, teachers and preachers, all you politicians,
We have a message to give you.

We all know a smiling face
Can make this world a better place.
We all know that each of you
Can make a friend today.

I'll Always Cherish Your Love

If we should meet in a café,
On a busy sidewalk, wink your eye, nod your head,
And let me know we're still friends.
When you talk about our past,
And our love and your friends,
Speak of me as the closest of them.
We were everything, every wish, every dream.
We shared a love in the comfort
Of a friendship fantasy.
If by chance you should call,
And need a friend,
Bet your life you can count
On me to understand.

Yes, I'll always cherish your love, my friend.

I can't go on playing this game of pretend,
I still love you like before.
Do you remember back then?
All your friends said it was so wrong,
They were blind and would not see.
It's not the skin that makes the man,
But the love that's beneath.

Yes, I'll always cherish your love, my friend.

If someone should ask about me,
Tell them I'm fine.
I don't mind doing time
In this lonely world of mine.
There are things I'd like to see
In the years when I'm old.

One is me, two is you,
Three is we're still friends.
I've got to stand up and dry my eyes
And keep myself strong.
Make a way to the top,
Make a life with my songs.
Take the time to open up
To what you feel inside.
You can be who you are,
If you would only try.

Yes, I'll always cherish your love, my friend.

I can't go on playing this game of pretend,
I still love you like before.
Do you remember back then?
All your friends said it was so wrong.
They were blind and would not see.
It's not the skin that makes the man,
But the love that's beneath.

Mary Goes Around

When Mary was a little girl,
She was touched by a haunted world.
In the night, she would bring to life
The secrets of her second sight.
In a world where they keep the dead
Their torment seemed to fill her head.
Her family remained unaware
Of the darker side of her gazing stare.
The spirits that she named as friends
Made them laugh at her games of pretend.
As Mary grew into a teen,
Her reality was lost in dreams.
She walked around with her head to the sky,
And everyone would wonder why.

Mary goes around and round,
Around and round, around and round again.
The voices keep calling, falling,
From her head as she spins,
Around and round, around and round,
Falling to the ground.
Mary rolls around and round
Around and round, around and round.
And as she tumbles, she mumbles
That only the voices know
Why Mary goes around and round.

Mary was placed in a special home.
They took away everything she owned.
They strapped her down in a padded room,
With cotton walls where sadness loomed.

The staff all said she was insane,
Locked in dreams inside her brain.
She spoke in rhyme and sang of death,
But they didn't know what Mary felt.

Years passed, and Mary ceased to dream.
She learned to talk about many things.
They placed her in a room with a view
Of a golden pond and morning dew.
The day came when they took her outside,
She ran toward the field; they wondered why.

Mary goes around and round,
Around and round, around and round.
The voices keep calling, falling,
From her head as she spins,
Around and round, around and round,
Falling to the ground.
Mary rolls around and round
Around and round, around and round.
And as she tumbles, she mumbles
That only the voices know
Why Mary goes around and round.

Once Upon

Once upon a dream, I found a lonesome thought
Behind my fantasies. Sweet memories it brought.
I saw your lovely face and touched your lips to mine.
I found a star to sit upon and watch you all the time.
Once upon a song, I found a love so strong,
Inside the melody we danced with hearts of stone.
A tear fell down and found a seed that grew a love affair;
Of faded eyes and silver lies that tarnished in despair.

Once upon, I wished upon
A lover's song, but now it's gone.
Once upon, I chanced upon
The moon and sun where love is born.
Once upon my memory,
You once were in love with me.

Once upon a burning love, I found a broken man.
His mended heart and promised love was broken once again.
His face design was that of mine from stories left untold,
Of secret dreams from days of old when heartaches unfold.
Once upon reality my life read like a book.
It revealed a sign in my mind where only few have looked.
Of a love so true that was introduced and played a part as friends.
Disguised with smiles and happy eyes, the story never ends.

Once upon, I wished upon
A lover's song, but now it's gone,
Once upon, I chanced upon
The moon and sun where love is born.

Once upon my memory,
You once were in love with me.

Faithful

You say you're searching for
Someone to give your love,
Someone to give your heart,
Someone to be a part
Of all of the things you feel inside.
That flow through your heart, and shine in your eyes.

It shows in your charm, it's there in your smile.
It's there in your touch, in your wonderful style.
So when you turn away
From all those words they say,
And there is no one who
Can give love that is true,
Just remember that I'm always around.
I'll never walk away, and I'll never let you down.

Faithful.
My heart has been conditioned
To be faithful.
Your love is my religion,
And I'm faithful,
Faithfully in love with you.

I'm faithfully in love with you.
No matter where you are,
I'll be your shining star,
I'll be your everything.
Just call on me
To be faithful,

Faithfully in love with you.
I'm faithfully in love with you.

You say you've searched so long,
To find a love that's strong,
To find a heart that's true,
For someone who will do
All the things that can make you feel
A never-ending need, a special kind of thrill,
A love inside burning bright as the sun,
A truth that shows you're their only one.
But if you ever find
Love that's a hurting kind,
That makes you sad and blue,
That breaks your heart in two,
Just call my name, and girl, I will be there.
I'll never stray away from your tender loving care.

Faithful.
My heart has been conditioned
To be faithful.
Your love is my religion,
And I'm faithful,
Faithfully in love with you.

I'm faithfully in love with you.
No matter where you are,
I'll be your shining star.
I'll be your everything.
Just call on me
To be faithful,
Faithfully in love with you.
I'm faithfully in love with you.

Locked Doors

The angel of the crystal pond
Prayed silently in the breaking dawn.
On bended knees I heard her weep,
Oh, Father, fill my soul with peace.
My words of love, let them fill your ears,
My sacrifice is these blood-stained tears.
Send me a sign, let your words be known
Lift up my heart to your heavenly throne.
She cried the tears for an unborn child,
Who never spoke, who never smiled.
Her prayers rang out to cleanse her soul
Of a sin that few will come to know.

There were chains around her mouth.
There was a shackle on her soul.
There was writing on the walls
That kept her behind locked doors.
I couldn't free her from her cage,
Or mend her wings that had been clipped.
There was redemption where she lay,
A taste of freedom on her lips.
Tell me, can you ignore
What goes on behind locked doors?

The angel of a morning star,
Knocked on Heaven's door at dark.
Her cry was heard through the galaxy,
Oh, Father, hast thou forsaken me?
These hands I've washed so many times,
To rinse away these sins of mine.
I lay me down at the golden gate.

I pray tonight my soul you'll take.
The unborn child she sought to find,
To cleanse her soul and free her mind.
Her prayers echoed through endless space,
For forgiveness for the sins she's made.

There were chains around her mouth;
There was a shackle on her soul.
There was writing on the walls,
That kept her behind locked doors.
I couldn't free her from her cage,
Or mend her wings that had been clipped.
There was redemption where she lay,
A taste of freedom on her lips.

Tell me, can I ignore
What goes on behind locked doors?

Walk into the Light

Finger on the trigger,
I've got a lie on my tongue.
There's nothing to consider
But to chamber the gun.
I don't want to live with me,
But I don't want to die.
I want to kill the beast in me,
That makes me hurt inside.
I tried to talk about it.
I tried to find some help.
But there's no way out of it,
When you're lost in yourself.

Shall I surrender to the pain I fight and
Walk into the light,
Where I won't feel the pain?
I'm never going to break these chains.
They're tightly wrapped around my heart.
I know it's going to be all right
When I walk into the light.

I hear my heart beating.
I count each breath I take.
My hand is hot and trembling.
In my heart there's an ache.
I don't want to say good-bye,
To be another memory.
But I must stop the fire inside
That burns endlessly.

Let a speeding bullet
End this emptiness.
This life I will forget,
When I'm laid down to rest.

I'll surrender to the pain I fight and
Walk into the light,
Where I won't feel the pain.
I'm never going to break these chains.
They're tightly wrapped around my heart.
I know it's going to be all right
When I walk into the light.

Taboo

There's a shake in the ground.
Hold onto your heart.
There's a fire all around,
And you're about to spark.
You better run for the ocean
To put out the flame,
To stop that devotion,
When he calls out your name.
There's a whisper in the wind
That seems to go nowhere.
Don't you listen to its sins;
Don't take the gifts he bears.

You walked on the water.
You had faith in his love.
You lay down at the altar.
The stars fell from above.
Pain became your master
As you mourned the loss
Of a chance forever after
To examine the cost.
Any fool but you
Could see that his love is taboo.

You better take higher ground.
Don't let it catch you sleeping,
Or surely you will drown.
When the love starts rising,
Don't think that you can swim.
There is no compromising,
When you give in to him.

There's a message on the wire,
But you need not reply.
It's the horns of his desires,
Burning in his white lies.

You walked on the water;
You had faith in his love.
You lay down at the altar.
The stars fell from above.
Pain became your master,
As you mourned the loss
Of a chance for ever after
To examine the cost.
Any fool but you
Could see that his love is taboo.

Baby Blue

I remember when I held your hand.
How good it felt to be your man.
Love was here, and love was alive.
I saw forever in your eyes.
I remember when I first held you
In a love that filled the room.

I never thought, I never realized,
That you'd be standing here saying good-bye.
When you left you took the best of love.
My mind will never forget your warm, tender touch.

Baby Blue,
My, my, my Baby Blue,
How I love you,
My, my, my Baby Blue.

You left a note to say good-bye.
I guess you didn't want to see me cry.
I tried so hard but I couldn't find you.
I just wanted to tell you that I love you.
Miles away, you called me from your car.
You said you had to follow your heart.

I never thought, I never realized,
That you'd be standing here saying good-bye.
When you left you took the best of love.
My mind will never forget your warm, tender touch.

You say you'll always be mine,
I love you, girl, until the end of time.
I just want to love you once again.

Whatever the price, I'm willing to sacrifice.
Parts of me are so mixed up,
But my heart still feels love.

I love you so much,
Baby Blue, Baby Blue,
How I love you,
My Baby Blue.
If you should ever need me,
I'll still be here waiting,
Baby Blue,
My Baby Blue.

Eve

I sat before a crystal ball.
Creation would pay the cost.
The fortune-teller gazed at me,
And said, "Come, fulfill your destiny."

I was taken back to an ancient time,
Placed in a garden that was so divine.
So perfect were the visual things,
My reality was someone's dreams.
Loneliness spares no one's heart.
You can think yourself a living God.
I wished away a part of me,
To feel her touching me tenderly.

Then in came Eve.
She led me to the tree of tranquillity,
And laid me down with hands of iniquity.
I was tempted by Eve
To taste the fruits of her ecstasy.
My eyes were opened, and now I see
That I'm not the first man she deceived.
Envy was the vanity of Eve.

The crystal ball ceased to reveal
The prophecy I came to hear.
Like opening Pandora's box,
The warmth of Eve filled my thoughts.
The serpent held the secret key
To unlock her sleeping vanity.
Her beauty was my greatest sin;
I worshipped it from deep within.

Her touch was like Saint Elmo's Fire;
It lit my heart with such desires.
What evil has made me confess
That I longed for her tenderness.

Then in came Eve.
She led me to the tree of tranquillity,
And laid me down with hands of iniquity.
I was tempted by Eve
To taste the fruits of her ecstasy.
My eyes were opened, and now I see,
That I'm not the first man she deceived.
Envy was the vanity of Eve.

Let's Fall in Love

Can I touch you, Baby?
Can I touch you there?
You know that I've been waiting
For this moment that we have.
If you could only see
All the love in me,
You'd open up your heart
And take me to ecstasy.
There's magic when I kiss you.
There's thunder in my heart.
You are the light in darkness
That shines from every star.
No, I would never leave,
Not while the love's in me.
I'm going to stay right here because
You are my destiny.

Because you know that I want you,
I know you want me too.
What else can we do
But fall in love?
Taking the chance again
To fall in love.
Finding romance again,
Let's fall in love.

I notice there's a sparkle
Of wonder in your eyes.
I know you're contemplating,
And it comes as no surprise
That you would want to be

Lying close to me,
Touching me like Heaven,
Loving me endlessly.
You know that I've been dreaming
That you would feel so right.
When you give in to love and
Surrender to the night.
No, you don't have to leave.
I've so much love in me.
You've got to stay right here 'cause
This is your destiny.

'Cause you know that I want you,
I know you want me too.
What else can we do
But fall in love,
Taking the chance again
To fall in love.
Chasing romance again,
Let's fall in love.

Look What God Can Do

Today I'm blessed that you've touched my life.
Today we'll be joined as husband and wife,
A union of love, friendship, and trust
A union that God has planned for us.
I need your strength, I need your love,
And I need your faith in God above.
I pledge my troth with all my heart
Till death do us part.

Look what God can do,
He made this love for me and you.
I give thanks for what He's done.
He took our hearts and made them one.
He gives to us this wedding day,
Assurance that He'll light our way.
He is the light; He is the truth,
Look what God can do.

I've learned to respect, I've learned to rely
On the love that shines in our eyes.
Love can inspire, love can breed scorn,
But faith separates the rose from the thorn.
So come take my hand and say "I do."
Accept God and me to walk beside you.
I'll cherish this day 'cause our love will serve
As the truth of God's word.

Look what God can do.
He made this love for me and you.
I give thanks for what He's done.
He took our hearts and made them one.

He gives to us this wedding day
Assurance that He'll light our way.
He is the light; He is the truth.
Look what God can do.

My Best Friend

Maybe when the lights are low,
She'll think about it.
Maybe then I'll hold her close,
But I doubt it.
I'm always there to sell her
On my words of passion.
She never let this be,
More than just my asking.
I'm not the one that
Holds her as a lover.
But with her I'm so relaxed,
And I know there's no other
Like my best friend.

She's my best friend.
I'll be there till the end.
Stormy weather, sunshine, or rain,
My love for her will never change.
All through the joy and pain
She's my best friend.

When I'm feeling down,
She's just a call away.
I know what we've found
Will last forever and a day.
She brings me so much joy
And fills a special need.

Sometimes I need more
Than her friendship can give.
But my heart can't ignore

That no one else makes me feel
Like my best friend.

She's my best friend.
I'll be there till the end.
Stormy weather, sunshine, or rain,
My love for her will never change.
All through the joy and pain
She's my best friend.

How to Miss You

In the first grade, back in school,
The teacher gave three simple rules:
We don't talk or play in class.
Raise your hand before you ask.
When I didn't know, I lied.
I guess that's just a schoolboy's pride.
Now I know what I should have learned:
Some bridges are better crossed than burned.

I can't learn how to miss you,
How to stop my heart
From falling apart.
They didn't teach us that in school,
How to turn loose
When love walks out on you.
No, they didn't teach us that in school,
What love puts us through,
And how to miss you.

When testing love we fail or pass.
Life's the teacher, we're the class.
If loving you were my final grade,
I didn't get quite what I gave.

I can't learn how to miss you,
How to stop my heart
From falling apart.
They didn't teach us that in school,
How to turn loose
When love walks out on you.
No, they didn't teach us that in school,

What love puts us through,
And how to miss you.

Learning how to live
With this heart that's still.
Trying to love without you,
Learning how it feels
To try to stop my tears
When I'm alone, missing you.

When It's Raining

Sunlight is never the reason
For these blues I fight.
It's nothing more than
Just a reason for night,
Where deep in dreams
She comes to me.
And, oh no, I'm thinking
About her face.
Where can I go
To bring back those yesterdays?

Sweet candlelight,
The passion of night,
The rain falling down on her skin.

When it's raining,
I surrender to her ghost
For the feeling
When she used to hold me close,
When it's raining,
Only when the rain comes down.

A rainy love, a soaking feeling
That she used to give,
Like rain falling down
On a parched field.
Her love was the bread
Of my soul.
I was such a fool
Who failed to be wonderful.

How did I lose
A love that was marvelous?

Sweet candlelight,
The passion of night,
The rain falling down on her skin.

When it's raining,
I surrender to her ghost
For the feeling
When she used to hold me close,
When it's raining,
Only when the rain comes down.

Oh no, I'm thinking
About her face.
Where can I go
To bring back those yesterdays?

Sweet candlelight,
The passion of night,
The rain falling down on her skin.

Social Graces

I'll take a stake
On the claim
To bring meaning
To my life,
Because I know
There's poverty
In the way
They think things are all right.

The issue isn't black or white,
It's how to solve this crime.
It's all about forgiveness,
Changing hearts and our old minds.
What we don't see isn't there.
What others do, we do not care.
Our children's children have been raised
To keep our families' secrets safe.

Well, those social graces,
Rules and places.
All they want to do is
Complicate my life.
They frisk me; they hit me;
And then they dismiss me.
They keep me guessing
When wrong is right,
When day is night.
Those social graces
In the damnedest places
All cause trouble in my life.

What a difference we can make
If we would cross that line
And admit we're all the same,
And it's all by God's design.
But we can't see what's not there.
What others do, we do not care.
Our children's children have been raised
To fight our war, to teach our faith.

Blacktop Fever

She was raised on freedom the country way,
Down in the heart of the USA.
She keeps a one-way ticket to paradise
Packed in her suitcase.
When she feels her heart a-hurting,
She sees the wheels a-turning,
Feels the road burning,
Deep within her soul.
She's got the key to open up new doors
That are waiting down the road.

Blacktop Fever, feet on the pedals
Of a one-ton diesel.
Like horses in a meadow,
She doesn't use a harness,
She rides without a saddle
When she races with the wind.
She breaks no laws
Till she turns on the speed.
She's a wanted girl.
She's just running free.
She's got a Blacktop Fever
That keeps her motor running,
A Blacktop Fever
That takes her everywhere.

White lines flowing, night and day;
Another town just drifts away.
If she stops to take a taste of life,
Would it be a big mistake?
So she keeps her wheels a-rolling,

Never really knowing,
Too afraid of slowing
To dream her life.
She's got a map that shows her every road,
But she doesn't know where to go.

Blacktop Fever, feet on the pedals
Of a one-ton diesel.
Like horses in a meadow,
She doesn't use a harness.
She rides without a saddle,
When she races with the wind.
She breaks no laws
Till she turns on the speed.
She's a wanted girl.
She's just running free.
She's got a Blacktop Fever
That keeps her motor running,
A Blacktop Fever
That takes her everywhere.

Deep into the city lights,
This country girl is going to burn out the nights.
She'll keep those big wheels turning,
Until she gets it right.

Car, Bars, Buses, Trains

Out on the open range
Beneath the stars, a cowboy sings,
Riding fences for my pay,
Growing older every day.

When I was a younger man
I had dreams, and I had plans:
A wedding ring, a wife, and kids.
Twice I promised I would quit.
She asked me not to up and go,
But a cowboy needs his rodeo.
So many miles, so many towns,
Letters seemed to dwindle down,
She said good-bye to loneliness,
The sweetest girl I ever met.

Those cars, bars, buses, trains,
Bringing me back home again,
Taking me straight to her love.
I hope she still believes in us.
Her faded picture in my vest
Is all I have to get her back,
To feel her love without the pain,
In these cars, bars, buses, trains.

Cars, bars, buses, trains,
Taking me back home again.

Six months ago, a broken man,
I packed my bag and quit the land.

All that I had left to show
Were scars left by the rodeo.

I still see her smiling face.
I often thought I'd find a trace.
A card, a call, a memory,
Some clue to where she might be.
The hand of fate is blind to love.
Sometimes we lose what never was.
Is she alone? Is she the same?
Has she taken someone's name?
I've got to find my way back home
To the sweetest girl I've ever known.

Those cars, bars, buses, trains,
Bringing me back home again,
Bringing me straight to her love.
I hope she still believes in us.
Her faded picture in my vest,
Is all I have to get back,
To feel her love without the pain,
In these cars, bars, buses, trains.
Bringing me back home again.

Hard to Let Go

I saw your sweet face.
I gave my heart away.
I gave my all
To share love with you.
You broke a perfect match.
Without you I'm only half
Of a love that's gone
That we once shared.

I'm not lonely.
I still think about you
Before the whiskey drowns
Away my blues.
Maybe everything now
Is all over,
But it's still too hard
To let go of you.

I saw you yesterday.
You took my breath away.
You still know how
To get next to me.
Another night to chase the past,
One more round for an empty glass,
For a love that's gone
That we once shared.

I'm not lonely.
I still think about you
Before the whiskey drowns
Away my blues.

Maybe everything now
Is all over,
But it's still too hard
To let go of you.

Stir it up, justify, lady.
Even you can't deny,
Without love we just survive,
Drowning in the whiskey and rye.
Who was right, who's to blame,
Whose heart hurts when love remains?
When letting go of you
Is the hardest pain.

I'm not lonely.
I still think about you
Before the whiskey drowns
Away my blues.
Maybe everything now
Is all over,
But it's still too hard
To let go of you.

Seventeen

We grow and we learn.
Sometimes we crash and burn
Searching for who we are,
In a world that's so unkind.
What we see and how we feel
Shapes the visions of our minds.

At seventeen we're kings and queens
In the glory of our prime.
We try to solve life's riddles.
We define who we are.
All things are considered
When we wish on falling stars.
Some will never have a choice
Or chances to rely
On the arms of someone's love
Or the hands of someone's pride.
All our roads have an end,
So dance while you can at seventeen.

For all the choices that we make,
There are promises to break.
There will be love and regrets
In our search for happiness.
Then all our lives
We'll chase those dreams
We dreamed as youths of seventeen.
Down those long and winding roads
That might have been.

For all the choices that we make
There might be promises we break.
There'll be love and some regrets
In our search for happiness.
Then all our lives
We'll chase those dreams
We dreamed as youths of seventeen.

Our roads have an end,
So dance while you can at seventeen.

Being Friends

People ask me how I know,
That I love you, why I glow.
What have we found that defies time,
A simple joy, a peace of mind?
You know why this love is real.
It's more than we are, more than we feel,
It's everything our hearts can share.
It's just the thought of being there.

Being friends
With the one you love
Is like living in
Heaven up above.
Where there are no tears
And there is no fear.
Where there are angels
Just like us,
Taking their time to be
So happy in love,
Being friends.

Every morning of every day
My every thought shines your way.
At times they roar, at times they flare.
Sometimes they're more than I can bear.
Yet you know why our love is strong.
It's faith in love that trust has grown.

Being friends
With the one you love,
Is like living in

Heaven up above.
Where there are no tears,
And there is no fear.
Where there are angels
Just like us,
Taking their time to be
So happy in love,
Being friends.

There are hearts
That wish on stars.
They hope to find
What we now know.
That being friends
Is how love grows,
Just being friends.

Call On Me

I have my own dreams, and
A faith that strengthens me.
You've shared my hand in prayer,
And it touched my heart with care.
At some time God chose to send
His blessing through the hearts of friends.
I'm thankful that He chose you
To teach His love and truth.

So if my hopes and dreams
All pass away,
Oh, friend, I'll be here for you.
Call me, call on me.
There nothing sweeter than
My need to tell you, friend,
How much, how much I'll miss you.
Call me, call on me.

My eyes glow with my hopes,
A lamp to light my roads.
Greater still is this bond of friends,
The honesty shared from within.
The hearts and souls you have touched
Have come to love you so much,
For they are seeds that have grown
By the light of God's throne.

So if my hopes and dreams
All pass away,

Oh, friend, I'll be here for you.
Call me, call on me.

There nothing sweeter than
My need to tell you, friend,
How much I love you.
Call me, call on me.

There's no road longer than a prayer,
No word greater than God's care.
I'll miss your smile while we're apart,
And have faith it's the will of the Lord.

So if my hopes and dreams
All pass away,
Oh, friend, I'll be here for you.
Call me, call on me.
There nothing sweeter than
My need to tell you, friend,
How much I love you.
Call me, call on me.

A Beautiful Sky

Morning comes,
And there's silence in the street.
The sunlight fills her room,
But she dares to take a peep.
There's something in their town,
That has changed their hearts to stone,
Bringing war upon their children,
Keeping them prisoners in their homes.

It brings tears to my eyes
When the innocence is lost
Of the child who has to pay
For the suffering we cause.
Oh, but look … What God has made:
Such a beautiful, beautiful sky.

With loving eyes
Every night she says a prayer
That when the sun rises
God has kept her in His care.
There's someone in her town
Who has sown the seeds of hate.
It's growing all around her,
On the fields where she once played.

Oh, but look … What God has made:
Such a beautiful, beautiful sky.

So much her eyes have shown me,
Even though she hardly speaks,

Of how God watches over us
Like every sparrow, every dove.

Oh, but look what God has made:
Such a beautiful, beautiful sky.

Spread your wings of faith and fly.
Come see His beautiful, beautiful sky.
Like every sparrow, every dove,
God watches over us.

Another falls,
A mother weeps.
Her son lies at her feet.
Yet she calls on God's love,
Every sparrow and dove.

Like every sparrow, every dove,
God watches over us.
Come see His beautiful, beautiful sky.

A Real Love

Well, you ask,
Who makes the rain,
And sunny days,
And birds that sing?
Who's the one
Who gave His life
For my sin?
Who has the right
To be a king,
And Prince of Peace?
Jesus has
But one belief:
The Father's love
We all should seek.
He is love.

In addition, you don't have to worry,
Because there will come a day
When all of the world
Will pass away.

A real love,
That's what Jesus is.
So full of life,
He gives me strength to live.
Then when I die,
I pray that my soul will bring
A chance to worship the King.

And next you ask
Who is this King?

What's the code?
Who has the key
To the soul?
Unlock the heart.
Jesus knows
Just who you are.
In the night,
In your darkest days,
He's the peace,
He's the only way.
He can heal and
Wash your sin away,
And He is Love.

You will see all there is to see,
You will know all there is to know,
You will feel all there is to feel,
For His love,
His love is so real.

A real love,
That's what Jesus is.
So full of life,
He gives me the strength to live.
Then when I die,
I pray that my soul will bring
A chance to worship the King.

Give Him Your Love

I see you there,
Wondering to yourself
If there's a cause,
For you to take a step,
And let Him into your heart.
But you know not where to start.
Well, all that He asks of us
Is that we give Him our love.

Jesus said, Please, for me,
Give Him your love.
He saved me on Calvary.
Why don't you give Him your love?

I've heard you say
You don't know how to change,
But the way that you are
Has brought you so much pain.
When you've fallen so low
That there's nowhere left to go,
There's someone who can pick you up
If you give Him your love.

Jesus said, Please, for me,
Give Him your love.
He saved me on Calvary.
Why don't you give Him your love?

Jesus died for you and me
On the cross at Calvary.

So give Him your love.

Why don't you give Him your love?

King of Kings

Who'll be left to pay
For the suffering of man?
There'll be hearts of little faith,
Praying with their hands of sin.
False tongues will call His name;
Every eye will see His face.
When His kingdom is proclaimed
The Earth will tremble in His grace.

King of Kings and Lord of Lords,
Mighty is my God.
King of Kings and Lord of Lords,
Mighty is my God.

The dead shall rise again,
A prophecy fulfilled.
When the last of His saints
Gather on the Shepherd's hill,
Death they shall not feel,
When their bodies are transformed
Into the spirit of His will,
Into the kingdom of His throne.

King of Kings and Lord of Lords
Mighty is my God.
Through the Son, Jesus Christ,
The victory is won.

From the clouds a mighty voice
Will shout *The King has come.*
With His vengeance he'll destroy
All the evil man has spun.

He will fill the lake of fire,
With the souls lost to sin,
Binding up the Devil's pride,
Bringing peace to Earth again.

King of Kings and Lord of Lords,
Mighty is my God.
Through the blood of Jesus Christ,
My victories are won.
King of Kings and Lord of Lords,
Holy is my God.
Through the Son, Jesus Christ,
Thy kingdom shall come.

Learning to Love

It seems to me that time
Is never enough.
We search all our lives
For someone we can trust.
We try to give our all,
To do the best we can.

I never thought that love
Would be such a friend.

Now I'm learning to love,
I'm learning to try,
I'm learning to trust
These feelings inside.
Because of you
My life has a page
In this book of love,
A book that we made.

Oh, if we could choose our lives
To be the very best,
Would the choices that we make
Ensure our happiness?
Still we try with all our hearts
To stop the sands of time?

I never thought that love
Would be a friend of mine.

Now I'm learning to love,
I'm learning to try,
I'm learning to trust

These feelings inside.
Oh, because of you,
My life has a page
In this book of love,
A book that we made.

My August Girl

Come aboard and let's set sail
For somewhere far away.
Where, I don't care,
'Cause I'd like to be
Sharing love
And drifting endlessly.
Let me show you
How sweet love can be.
The stars and the moon
Will guide us
To ecstasy.

My August girl,
So beautiful and fine,
You're truly Nature's best
Creation and design.
Midnight stars are in your eyes,
Sunshine in your smile.
Summer is the feeling
That I feel inside,
My August girl.

Summer days bring to mind
The beauty of this love inside.
It's a joy, so warm, so rare.
In you I've found
The bright sunshine,
A song, a perfect rhyme.
I will sing

And I will dream of
Your love for eternity.

Summer is a feeling,
That I feel inside.
I wish I had your loving, girl,
Wish that you were mine,
My August girl.

My August girl,
So beautiful and fine,
You're truly Nature's best
Creation and design.
Midnight stars are in your eyes,
Sunshine in your smile.
Summer is the feeling that I feel inside,
My August girl.

Fairy Tales

Well, that look that's on your face,
The thought that you are wearing
Cannot be replaced
By the way that I feel.
I should have your heart;
I should have your loving.
If only you believed
In things that should be.
I know that I've been dreaming
To keep myself afloat,
Loving you in fairy tales,
Fantasies, and hopes.
How long does forever last
When storybooks are all we have?

The children laugh,
The children cry,
We tell some truths,
We tell some lies.
I know what it is to fantasize,
In fairy tales that never die.

Morning comes, skies are gray,
Will it rain? Who's to say?
We all like those sunny skies,
Lazy days and butterflies.
Skipping stones and jumping rope,
Playing tag and passing notes.
Funny things done as a child
Can still bring a smile.
Somewhere we lost faith;

We let life change our ways.
We let it take away the magic
That our fantasies can make.
If I could turn this heart around,
Believe that what's lost can be found,
I know that I could be whatever
Your heart needs me to be.

Well, I'd like to believe in fairy tales,
And more than a wish in wishing wells.
I'd like to believe in rainbow's gold,
And how love is supposed to go.
I'd like to believe two hearts that are true
Can become the dreams I dream with you.
I'd like to believe that fairy tales
Are not just for the children's play.

Sing the way the children sing.
Play the way the children play.
Live life as you dream it to be.
Believe in what you say.

Drawing pictures in the sand
And feeling so carefree,
I keep on playing in this playground
Where the children still believe,
All the stories have happy endings,
And love changes all things.
I keep on looking for the magic
That would bring your heart to me.

Something (Lost in a Whisper)

I lost in a whisper
Something that tickles,
Something that triggers love.

When I'm running hot and cold,
Girl, I just want to chase that ghost.
Within the walls of private talk,
Until I'm outlined in white chalk,
I'll reach for the peak and climb
High up on this love design.
Mine will never be a love that's
Denied a parking sign.

Something about the way it flows,
A little something
About the way you've got me
Going through these doors
And this lockdown chills my soul.

Something,
Really something,
Has got me pumping,
Keeps me jumping.
Lost in a whisper,
Something,
Really something,
Has got me pumping,
Keeps me jumping.

Girl, when I call out your name,
Those silent whispers seem insane.
The way it's read, in my bed,

There's nothing for the quick or dead.
Don't stay for the pony ride,
The puppet show in love's disguise.
I would never pull the string,
If I didn't want the bell to ring.

Something
About the way it flows,
A little something
About the way you've got me
Going through these doors
And this lockdown chills my soul.

Something,
Really something,
Has got me pumping,
Keeps me jumping,
Lost in a whisper.

Twister, Twister

There's a twister coming, Baby.

Are these stolen feelings?
Is this the perfect crime?
Where do I run for cover
When the storms are in my mind?
A man who has no courage
Against a jealous wind
Will tremble inside
When the storms of love begin.

The Twister will come,
And it tears apart
All the things I built
In this house of love.
I try to live
In the winds of change.
I try to hold my ground
When he calls your name.

Twister, Twister,
Turns inside,
Stirring up my jealous pride.
Angrily I say these things
To hurt the one
Who wears my ring.

What of the moments after,
When these feelings can't find peace?
In your eyes there's a shelter,
And your smile comforts me.
How many rescues are there

Within your tender heart?
How many more forgiveness's
Does it take to light the dark?

When I'm storming out,
When I'm locked down on this feeling,
Show me what this love's about,
Because I want to know.

The Twister would come,
And it tears apart
All the things that I built
In this house of love.
So I try to live
In the winds of change.
I try to hold my ground
When he calls your name.

Twister, Twister,
Turns inside,
Stirring up my jealous pride.
Angrily I say these things
To hurt the one
Who wears my ring.

ESP

Now that there's love
Inside of me
(I want to be loved),
All I need is ESP.
(I'll never give you up.)

I do care about the way
You feel inside.
I can't hide
All the love.
It's what keeps me alive.

If you feel like you can fly,
I'll be your wings in the sky.
I wish I could show you
How this love is gonna be.
Wish I had a little ESP.

Now that there's love
Inside of me
(I want to be loved),
All I need is ESP.
(I'll never give you up.)

Somewhere, where the water flows,
There's so much that's unknown.
Baby, with your love inside,
I'm never going to be alone.
Love can be so real.
I know why you should feel

There's more than love inside of me.
Must be a little ESP.

Now that there's love
Inside of me
(I want to be loved),
All I need is ESP.
(I'll never give you up.)

Your eyes are so beautiful.
You're as pretty as can be.
I cannot go back, no,
To how we used to be.
Love we can have forever,
One moment at a time.
What can it be but miracles,
That make me believe you're mine.

Now that there's love
Inside of me,
(I want to be loved)
All I need is ESP.
(I'll never give you up)

Six * Sex

Oh girl,
You know I've been dreaming about you.
I've been thinking about you lying next to me and
Making love and
Showing you the six ways of loving,
The six ways, and the six days.

Six * Six * Six * Six * Sex,
I've got real love
That you won't forget.
You won't forget.

Baby, I've been watching you,
Forever and a day.
The way you move,
That body, girl,
It just blows me away.
I know one plus one is two,
And the sum is you and me,
It takes you * me * love * us,
To teach you how to multiply.

Six * Six * Six * Six * Sex,
I've got real love
That you won't forget.
You won't forget.

I want you lying next to me
With the lights soft and low.
The taste is sweeter,
So much deeper,
When your loving starts to flow.

I want to rub your body up and down
Until you want me inside.
All the things that I do to you, girl,
Is what it is to multiply.

Oh, six ways, six days,
Hugging, touching, kissing, rubbing,
Tasting your sexy body.
I'll put you in the mood,
Make you want to feel the groove.
Six * Six * Six * Six * Sex,
I've got real love
That you won't forget.
You won't forget.

Weeping Willow

I'm going to weep
Like a weeping willow,
Baby, you won't see my tears.
I'm going to weep
Like a weeping willow,
Crying down through the years.

Come into my dreams.
Let me show you fantasies.
What I thought was real
Is what I thought that you would feel.

I gave my heart and soul forever,
Hoped that love would start to grow,
But you just told me I was dreaming.
I just want to know, Baby,
Why you're so cold,
When I know that your heart
Can give me so much more.

I'm going to weep
Like a weeping willow.
Baby, you won't see my tears.
I'm going to weep
Like a weeping willow,
Crying down through the years.

Words left in silence,
Dreams that once were everything,
Don't save me.
As the willow grows,
I'm hanging on to every hope

That come tomorrow we're together
And this love is so real.
Won't you touch me and love me, Baby.
I don't need to know
Why is it that you're so cold
When I know that your heart
Can give me so much more.

I'm going to weep
Like a weeping willow.
Baby, you won't see my tears.
I'm going to weep
Like a weeping willow,
Crying down through the years.

When the willow bends in the wind
And life begins again,
I hope that you and I
Will be more than friends.
If you trust in what I'm feeling,
Feel the love inside of me,
Then you will see.
Tell me why it has to be
That I weep
Like a weeping willow.
Baby, you can't see my tears.
I'm going to weep
Like a weeping willow,
Crying down through the years.

This Kind of Happiness

Around and round I go,
Riding on this carousel
Of dreams that won't let go.
'Cause you know I've been waiting for
Your love, heart, and soul.

I'm hooked on this feeling,
So happy in love,
'Cause I know
This kind of happiness
That I feel inside
Is so wonderful.
It keeps me feeling high.

What I feel for you
Is the deepest love
That two hearts can feel.
And it's just for us.

Thinking of your smile,
Eyes that take me to forever
On dreams of here and now.
Your beauty keeps me in this Heaven.
I'm never coming down.

I'm hooked on this feeling,
So happy in love,
'Cause I know
This kind of happiness
That I feel inside

Is so wonderful.
It keeps me feeling high.

What I feel for you
Is the deepest love
That two hearts can feel,
And it's just for us.

This kind of happiness
I've been looking for,
This kind of happiness
Keeps me wanting more.

In and out and in between,
Love keeps me wanting more.
Kiss me once, I'll feel it twice.

This kind of happiness,
I've been looking for,
This kind of happiness
Keeps me wanting more.

Such a wonderful feeling
I've got being close to you.
Girl, you know there's nothing else
I would rather do
Than hold you close to me
And share your tender love.
Baby, can't you see
It's you I'm dreaming of.

This kind of happiness
That I feel inside,
Is so wonderful.
It keeps me feeling high.

What I feel for you
Is the deepest love
That two hearts can feel,
And it's just for us.

Butterfly

Such a beautiful song
My Butterfly sings
As she opens up her wings.

You will always be
My pretty Butterfly,
Flying in the sky,
With summer in your eyes.

You're my first rainbow of joy,
My heavenly sunrise.
I know that I am truly blessed
To walk with you down this aisle.

So beautiful when they arrive,
Butterflies, Butterflies,
A bundle of joy, a father's pride,
Butterflies, Butterflies,
One day they'll fly away.

What a sight to see,
My pretty Butterfly,
Dancing on a breeze,
Laughing as she flies.
The years have gone too fast,
She's come to fly away.
I'm so proud she asked
To walk with me this day.

Fly, Fly, my Butterfly,
Fly, Fly into the sky.

Fly; Fly, my Butterfly,
Fly high into the sky.

I have come to see
My pretty Butterfly,
Open up her wings
And fly into the sky.
I love the way you smile,
The woman you've become.
If loving tears have filled your eyes,
You're not the only one.

So beautiful when she arrived,
My Butterfly, my Butterfly.
My bundle of joy, my father's pride,
My Butterfly, sweet Butterfly.
I know she'll fly away
From me
On this very day.

Fly, Fly, my Butterfly,
Fly, Fly into the sky.
Fly, Fly, my Butterfly,
Fly high into the sky.

Just Like This

On a day like this
I'll remember you,
So beautiful in love,
A fairy tale come true.
If time could stop for us,
If we could frame this day,
We'd forevermore
Want to love this way.

Just like this,
Forever I want to be.
Just like this,
Loving you tenderly.
Like the sparkles in our eyes,
Like the magic when we kiss,
Love will keep us all our lives
Just like this.

On a night like this
We'll celebrate our love.
Everyone will gather round.
I will only see
The smile upon your face
For a life of love,
For the promises we made.

Just like this,
Forever I want to be.
Just like this,
Loving you tenderly.
Like the sparkles in our eyes,

Like the magic when we kiss,
Love will keep us all our lives
Just like this.

Touched by the Visitors

Is Heaven where souls will find peace
When Earth and time have ceased to be?
Is it wisdom that holds the key
To unlock life's mysteries?
There's a place that I've seen,
Where death begins a life of dreams.
The truth revealed: our souls are beings.
They are living entities.
When you wish upon a star,
The dreams you dream can take you far
Beyond this life through open doors
To the home of Visitors.

Look beyond the skies,
Where Heaven serenades Earth,
Beneath the stars of Venus,
Looking in their eyes,
I find the meaning
For the Visitors.

I can hear them calling
When night starts falling.
I can hear them coming,
Coming for me tonight.

They're secrets that lie deep in your mind,
Living between the truth and lies.
They ease your mind but trouble your soul.
You pretend that you don't know.
You try to free your soul from pain,
But the thoughts drive you insane.

It doesn't feel good, but it doesn't feel bad,
Being touched by the Visitors.

I can hear them call my name
Deep in the night. They sound so strange.
Voices echo through my brain,
Speaking to me, but not in words.
There's nothing to stop them when they appear.
They take you into your darkest fears.
You can't believe that they're for real
Until you're touched by the Visitors.

Here comes the light that can take control.
It's a part of me that can't let go.
It fills me until I want to know
The touch of the Visitors.
As in a dream, I try to wake.
I try to scream, but no one hears.
Then I know I must accept
The touch of the Visitors.

Look beyond the skies,
Where Heaven serenades Earth,
Beneath the stars of Venus.
Looking into their eyes
I find the meaning
Of the Visitors.

Burning Up

Burning up, I'm burning, burning, burning up,
I'm burning, burning, burning up.
I want to make love to you.

911, help me please,
I cannot breathe,
She's so damn hot,
This is an emergency.
The way she walks,
Makes me break into a sweat.
I'm so turned on.
I'm not even ready yet.
Her sexy smile
Grabs me like a heart attack.
Please bring my wine,
Because I know where the party's at.

Burn, Baby, burn, Baby, burn, Baby, burn.
Burn, Baby, burn, Baby, burn.
Burning up, I'm burning, burning, burning up,
I'm burning, burning, burning up.
I want to make love to you.

411, give me
Information please.
Who can I call
About this fire inside of me?
It's burning wild.
I'm about to lose control.
Somebody said that wisdom is worth much more than gold.
Who is this girl

That got me in this fantasy?
Please place this call,
'Cause this is an emergency.

Burn, Baby, burn, Baby, burn, Baby, burn
Burn, Baby, burn, Baby, burn, Baby, burn
Burning up, I'm burning, burning, burning up,
I'm burning, burning, burning up.
I want to make love to you.

When I'm burning up with desire,
The thought of you makes me hotter.
Come a little closer to this fire.
Let these flames of love take us higher.

Burning up, I'm burning, burning, burning up,
I'm burning, burning, burning up.
I want to make love to you.

My skin's on fire
At a thousand degrees.
The heat is rising,
And I cannot breathe.
Somebody help me.
Pour some water on me,
'Cause I'm burning.
Can this be ecstasy?

Dawn

Hang up the gloves,
Count me out to ten.
The title is yours.
There's nothing left to defend.
Victory tastes like Heaven,
Joyful in the tears that fall.
One more round of confusion and
The winner takes all.

Dawn, you're heavy,
Too heavy to carry.
Dawn, you're heavy.
Will you lighten the load?

You were born a star.
You came to fill my skies.
Still, stars fall sometimes.
Burning truths, burning lies,
Dawn, don't try to pace me.
My endurance is at end.
One more round of loneliness.
We're losing as friends.

Dawn, you're heavy,
Too heavy to carry.
Dawn, you're heavy.
Will you lighten the load?

Your Love Is Where I Belong

I'd like to be
All your desires
Burning in the midnight sun.
I'd like to be the one
To cool down the fire
When you know the heat is on.

I'm hanging on, strung out on emotions.
I'm giving you this heart of mine.
Just do things
That make me feel a part of your
Every mood, your every day now.

And if I'm ever down on luck,
I'll need a love like yours
To win again.
I don't want to lose your love
If there is a magic drug
To make you feel all lost in love.
I'm high again,
So high that I know
Your love is where I belong.

Your love is deep,
Cool as a river
That flows gently on my mind.
I'll be there,
Swimming in your loving,
Every time your eyes meet mine.

I want your love, body, soul, and spirit,
To be as one within our hearts.

Just give me
Your sweet, sweet surrenders.
Just give me your ways of loving.

And if I'm ever down on luck,
I will need a love like yours
To win again.
I don't want to lose your love
If there is a magic drug
To make you feel all lost in love.
I'm high again,
So high that I know
Your love is where I belong.

978-0-595-67822-8
0-595-67822-X

Printed in the United States
88543LV00007B/14/A